The Way Butterflies Look At Flowers

2

Attention

Their glasses touched one another with a
      familiar chime
A look from him
A wink from her
Allowing a giggle at her gesture would have been
      inappropriate, but a grin
        that slowly curved into a coy smile
      was firmly maintained
He brought the glass towards his mouth
And at the moment that the fermented fluid
      touched his lips
She silently brushed the inside of his left pant leg
      with the top of her right foot
His eyes widened as he lowered the chalice
      to the tabletop before
      calmly focusing his gaze upon her
Leaning back in her seat
She allowed her eyes to ever so obviously
      look down towards her lap
      parting her knees underneath the table
Their eyes met again and she savored the
      change in his stare
Now that she had his attention

One

Eyes close
Memories of previous nights flood her
Taking her to where he can always be
       around her
       inside of her
       one with her
To a place where afterwards they lay
       under starry skies
Making wishes they each dreamed of telling
       one another
Lips remaining quiet so that the sanctity of
       their yearnings would remain intact
Theirs to keep in the silent hope for fruition

Umbrella

I wanted to be her umbrella and
      keep her out of the rain
But somehow
All I seemed to do was continue to
      make her wet

Precursors

The peppering of ever deepening kisses
   on her delicious lips throughout the
   dancing we did in the living room
   were solidified precursors to the
   impatient fucking
   that would soon take place
   in the kitchen

Tapping

It had been on her mind throughout the day
    his ridges being forced across her lips
    and tongue
The look in his eyes after she stepped
    through the door
She pushed him against the wall
    dropped to her knees and
    sucked him dry
Looking up at his eyes, she blinked
And as she did her tongue dashed his
    precious release
    down her throat before
    turning her head and
    resting the side of her face on his
    still throbbing tissue
The pulse of a softening body exhaustively
    tapping on the skin of her cheek
All before she had spoken a single word

April

The gaze they were lost in kept her flowers watered
without the showers of April

Brushstrokes

Looks

Whispers

Pressure

Rotation

Growls

All the brushstrokes I used to paint the masterpiece
      that forces her to cum
      while fully clothed

A Warm Bath

He held his lover tightly
    with hands interlocked
    behind her back
She sighed
Laying a weary head onto
    comforting shoulders while
    her breasts pressed against him
Sinking into his soothing embrace
    as one would
    slip into a warm bath

Hard to Breathe

I inhaled her for she provided
  so much more than the air to me
I was enamored by the way
  she filled my lungs and
  made it hard for me to breathe

I would gasp for her and
  repeatedly draw her in
The fire she brought from me
  altered my chemistry and
  swelled my veins with sin

Ready to Dream

Thunder sounded
Sometimes subtly
Sometimes startlingly
Always bringing a smile or a
      sleepy, pleasant thought
      as we lay intertwined
      throughout the night
Finding joy in the storm beyond the windows
Even after the storm that brought such rain
      from our bodies
      had left us exhausted and
      ready to dream

Dissonance

Upon his being spent she feels his pulse
      inside of her

Patiently waiting

He slides from her
      adorns the boxer briefs that laid
      on the floor and
      exits the room
Off to replenish the fluids lost
      amidst their lovemaking
When his feet cross the threshold of the doorway
      she slides a hand under
      body temperature sheets
Laying it between open legs as a receptacle
      for the soft warmth that slowly
      fills the spaces
      between her fingers before bringing it up to
      her lips

It is then that she
        closes her eyes
        separates her lips and
        allows the flavor of their
        passion to
        dance across her tongue
Like the sound of a dissonant chord flows
        across ones ears
Savoring the result of the way they had
        loved each other
        only moments before

This was her time

Starving

She wanted to touch him
    with everything that forced
    her to breathe
The rope around her wrists
    made it clear that her fingertips
    were to be left hungry
Each time he forcefully entered her
    fingers held themselves
    tighter and tighter
Starving for the same grip that
    his hands had upon her flesh

Any Time of Day

She taught me that I didn't need to be
      under a night sky
      to see the stars
When I closed my eyes she could
      bring them to me
      at any time of day

Unrewarded

Head on a pillow
His eyes open to the absence of light
      expected at 2:13am
Awoken by a throbbing between his legs
      and a frenzy of thoughts that
      must have been
      leftover fragments of a
      dream about her
He swallowed silently and swore he could
      taste her skin
He was left with no choice but to
      relieve himself
      at that very moment
Because dreams like these should never go
      unrewarded

A Moment Ago

The meeting of lips precedes the
      extending of his tongue
Firmly and slowly it circles around her
All but forcing her body back into the mattress
      as fingers gripped the sheets at her sides
The fact that they had finished
      only a moment ago
      was evident by the ease at which
      two fingers slid into her
      underneath his chin and the
      softening between his legs
She tasted bright like sunshine as he occasionally
      dropped his tongue lower to
      savor the adoration
      he had filled her with
Before tasting harder
      twisting his hands and coaxing
      her voice to release into his ears
      the way her body delighted his mouth

Threshold

Reaching behind
She wrapped her hand around the
    damp
      still firm piece of him
      that was only a moment ago
      pumping inside of her
She held his head firmly against
      a threshold he had never crossed
Making circles around her unfucked ass
All while wiggling a curious backside like the
    flame from a candle
    on a drafty winter's evening
While he silently begged for her to tenderly
    set him ablaze

Phonograph

Neither a stylus am I
     nor vinyl are you
But the audio that results from my needle
     dragging effortlessly through your grooves
     plays as my favorite song

Accompaniment

Falling alongside my lover as a
      drowning man who has
      fought his way to shore
Exhausted and heavy arms pull me
      to where I collapse upon the sand
An ear at the center of her chest
Laying ever still as I try to decide
      which is more
The pressure of the heart
      beating inside me, or
      the pounding of hers against my cheek
Arms envelop me, and in doing so
      a soft breast is brought to
      embrace my face
I kiss the sweat-tinged skin and
      quietly enjoy the accompaniment
      of the hearts and lungs
      underneath our flesh

Streetlamp

The beauty of the body she presented me
Skin gently bathing in the warm light
    from the streetlamp
    just outside the open window
Outshined only by her voice gently
    falling upon my ears
    begging me to fuck her

Eden

The sins of the moment
     render her cries to God as
     blasphemous
Holiness is not to be found between these sheets
There is no Eden here

Empty

Legs open
Presenting unto me a paradise
    where I
        feast without becoming full
    where I
        stay warm despite exposed skin
    where I
        become lost in her eyes
        while feeling at home
        as I
        drain myself into her
        without ever feeling empty

Drowned

They drowned in
        themselves
In each other
Neither wanting to come up for air

Campfire

To him she was like a campfire
Bright
Cozy
Mesmerizing
She took the chill from the
     cool
       damp air that surrounded him
How he loved being wrapped in her warmth

Unexpected

Cries of bliss are muffled by my
      open mouth
An attempt to keep the sounds she makes
      while soaking me
      from falling upon the ears of
      unexpected guests

Hands

If your hands never close around me
If they never repeatedly
     fold and tighten
     this layer of skin
If your delicate knuckles are never
     licked clean from the flow
     of my bliss
Why be born with them at all?

Waste

What a waste to have so much skin
    while I am too far away to touch you

Leather Sofa

His right hand ran through her hair
     while his left stroked
     her face
     neck and
     chest
Occasionally wandering comfortably over the
     breasts within his reach
She lay on the leather sofa with her head in his lap
     talking about her day as
     his hands pampered her
During the silent moments her eyes fought
     to stay open
     as tender fingers relaxed her into
     a space so near slumber
All he wanted was to be and enjoy her peace

Opportunity

He had laugh lines
    crows feet and
    gray hair at his temples
Smiling gently
    he firmly took her hand in his
    over the table at which they sat
    stroking her with his thumb
Looking up
    their eyes met and she silently remarked
    to herself that those eyes
    seemed to devour her
She could hardly wait to grant his lips
    the same opportunity

So Softly

Whenever she walked past she would
     whisper her darkest desires into the
     invisible ears of her favorite flowers
Always were they listening but
     so softly did they speak
The wind at times so eager to help would
     carry their responses to her nose
     so she might inhale what they
     had to say

Breath with Purpose

A long drawing of air is commenced before
    being released to produce
      the cries of ecstasy my mind was determined
      to drag from her body

A breath with purpose

We Owned the Night

Repeatedly gasping under the clutches of
    one another
    we owned the night
The full moon illuminating the room enough to
    allow my eyes the shadow-laden view
      of her form as my fingers pushed deeper
      into her
She rocked against my grip before
    letting herself go
And for a moment
The cares our hearts toil so tediously over were
    cast aside into the cold of a winter's night
This fleeting moment in time a possession of only
    the gifted and the giver

Crashing

Ebbs and flows

Natural

Autonomous

She moves against the stroking of my hand with
      the enrapturing motion of the sea

My eyes the sun
Filling hers with light into a blue lunar beauty
      that becomes full

Pulling the tide below to
      spill over my hands as
      the ocean crashing upon the shore

Flooded

Her mind was always flooded with thoughts of
　　　the way he kissed her
Kisses that occupied her mouth
As other lips were
　　　cupped
　　　opened and
　　　kissed
The way only his hands ever could

Circles

The tips of frail eyelashes
    land on soft cheeks as
    a brow begins to wrinkle before
    her mouth opens and those lips
    take the shape of the circles
    my adoring fingers turn
    under her panties

Wind Through Grass

No sight from the scarf gently tied around
      her eyes
Mouth held open by a ball that her lips
      nervously surrounded
She knew he was always there
      she could hear him
      she could smell him
Combining her available senses she knew he had
      placed himself on the opposite side
      of the gag
And for a moment, but yet a lifetime
      she swore she could taste him
Fingertips moved through her hair
      like wind blowing through grass
      on a summer's day
      as these hands freed her tongue
      from its prison
A tear nearly fell from a blink
      as she greedily feasted upon him in an effort
      to satisfy a hunger she never knew she had

Dots

The polka dots she wore drove me crazy
To me, each decorative circle merely represented
    a spot on her skin that my mouth was
    dying to taste

Petrichor

Accompanied by wandering hands
   slightly calloused and
   strong from years of labor
His lips touched the knees exposed by
   the length of her sundress
The only sights that he registered were the
   backs of his eyelids
   as kisses moved ever higher
Along the fabric that met his face mid-thigh
   a gentle hand was placed at each of
   his temples
Deliberately guiding her lover's mouth to rest
   upon the skirt draped between her
   fair skinned hips
A tensing between his legs followed the inhaling
   of her petrichor
An ache that would soon be relieved as this was
   only the beginning of their storm

Lilac

Tree at her back
    sun in her hair
Lilac breezes decorate
    the scent of the air

She digs into the grass
    with the softest bare feet
Hoping in her heart that someday again
    they'll meet

Keep Us Warm

I secretly keep the room cold at night
    to ensure that she holds me close and
    tucks the blankets
    tightly around our skin
To keep us warm
    all through our slumber

Independence Day

Streaks of fire lit the sky
> before the sizzle and report
> landed upon her ears

He wrapped his arms around her
> as they enjoyed the
> holiday display

After flickering sky-lit kisses her thoughts strayed
> to the way he tasted in her mouth
> earlier that afternoon

And how she wished he was exploding
> inside of her

Reach

Her jaw dropped slowly for me

A level tongue invites me between parted teeth
  as my first two fingers grow warmer the
  further they reach beyond her open lips

Fingerprints slide across a wet tongue as the
  tips of my fingers rest where that very
  tongue begins to fall into her throat and
  where a soft uvula rests between my nails

Lips wrap around me before she closes her eyes
  and moans quietly as she sucks and licks

Inspiring me to swell and stiffen before
  removing my fingers
  standing and
  presenting her with another
  part of me to wrap those
  darling lips around

Drought

The kisses she planted near his knees
    were like the softly speaking thunder
    of an approaching atmospheric disturbance
Boisterous clouds slowly made their way
    up his thigh
Leaving a sprinkling of the impending rain
    each time her lips pressed against his skin
The darkness of her thickening cloud cover
    settled over him
There she sucked like a summer storm
    hot and
    humid
The thunder of her voice sighing against skin that
    she loved to taste
Triggered the downpour that rained behind
    a sealed mouth
Relieving the drought of a dry, thirsty tongue

Quenching

Warm fluid falling
Quenching my thirst with water
Trickling from her breasts

Ivy

Slowly and deliberately her hand did move
Like ivy searching for a place that it could see
      the sun
She enjoyed the weight of him
Holding his enamoration for her
      within her hand
A grasp closed upon him
      as he continued to swell
Watching his veins collapse and give way
      under the deliberation of her fingers was
      pure joy
With a painfully slow increase of speed
      she pulled the skin in her grip
      away from and towards his body
Repeating with intention
His body unconsciously followed
      her graceful movements
      as the tide unknowingly obeys the moon
He erupts
She smiles

Slightly dropping her jaw as
        the sunshine of her efforts
        feeds her botanic hunger
A second hand joins in an attempt to
        capture his flow like a jealous branch
Both feeding and nourishing the same

Hotel Pool

The water was all around us
Every sound echoed from the concrete that
      enclosed the room
It was only her and I
We drenched ourselves in both warm and
      cool waters
Our mouths smiling and speaking of how
      good it felt
      to be away
She wrapped legs and arms around me
      as I easily elevated her nearly
      weightless body
Holding her against me with submerged hands
      satisfied to be feasting on her ass
Between kisses I would catch sight of
      water droplets sliding down
      strands of hair only to
      disappear on her skin
I lifted and carried her from end to end
The way she deserved to be
      lifted and cradled
The way I do in my dreams

Pedicel

I longed for the touch of her hands for the same
      reasons flowers needed sunlight
The skin she laid upon me warmed this body
      as if it was comprised of outstretched
      leaves that were desperate for ultraviolet
      sustenance
This, along with the moisture she willingly rained
      upon me guaranteed a
      firm
      lengthening
      healthy pedicel
And enough nectar to gratify any thirst

Summer Always Is

If I could just once fall from the warm clouds
      above you
Through hair that clings to fair skinned cheeks
Between neck and shirt collar
Across the space between your nipple and bra
Through the invisible hairs of your navel
      to where you hide behind a zipper and
      dainty undergarments
Where summer always is

Mariposa

Delicate legs at each of my hips
She lowers onto me
> with the apparent warmth and ease
> accommodated by genuine
> predetermination
Landing on me as if I were a flower
Her arms on my neck as my hands are
> ever elsewhere
She pushes against me with a determined rhythm
One that grows in pressure and tempo
> before my fingers grip her gorgeous hair
> pulling her face from my shoulder
Her mouth opens and closes as if it were wings
> of a butterfly
Before she
> slows
> softly whimpers
> stops and
> slides down my lap
Where with frail fingers and lips flexing like
> swallowtail wings
She takes every drop of nectar I give

Simply Smile

She watched with a curious gaze and refused
    to keep herself from being included
    in the interaction
Wrapping fingers around him to help their guest
    she followed his lips as if her
    thumb and forefinger were connected
    to his mouth

Redrawing the lines of their friendship
    with each passing second
A new experience for each
    enjoyed by all three

The sight of her man in the mouth of another
    allowed hers to do something
    previously impossible
    as he enjoyed the sensation

Simply smile

A smile that grew into a devilish grin
    with the thoughts
    of the things she could have them both
    do to her
    while naked in the room together

It was time for her to become the
    center of attention

Cotton Candy

Sweat glistens and
    breathing is deep
Her voice weak and weary as I
    peer into infatuated eyes

Trapped in her gaze
    like laying upon the grass in mid-July
Losing myself in the sight of
    cotton candy skies

Wildflower

They took steps through the
    knee-high grass
Fingers intertwined
Admiring the seemingly random placement
    of the flowers that surrounded them
Bringing each other's attention to
    blossoms that would catch one's eye
Finding joy in the bumblebees that hovered
    from bloom to bloom
His mind in a meadow where he could
    immerse himself into his
    wildflower
If only to become coated in things far sweeter
    than nectar and pollen

Painful Restraint

Hair is brushed aside as my lips meet the
        back of her neck
Her hands drop to the counter she stands
        in front of
Approval is shown by the pushing back against me
        and the wiggling of her backside
        against my zipper
Forcing me to use painful restraint to keep from
        reaching down
        grabbing that adorable ass
        spreading it and
        fucking her there

Gifter

I need for you to open your
      mouth
      legs and
      soul
For everything I have to give to you

Hunter

Strong fingers release a string
Sending the arrow of his commanding gaze
    in her direction
She falls onto cool sheets as a fawn would
    onto a late autumn meadow
Without a struggle she lay and a gasp races
    from her mouth
As she gives him what he wishes to take

Cherry Blossoms

Porcelain skin
     a blank canvas begging for color
Impacts and grabbing leave the
     visual impression of a
     flowering garden comprised of
     distorted pastel handprints
Hundreds of hands blanket her
     providing a weightless duvet of pink
     upon her fair complexion
When all is done she stands
     in front of the mirror and
     smiles at what she has become
All she sees are the cherry blossoms of May
     while the springtime that brought
     them into bloom
     silently dreams underneath
     the softest of sheets
     on the bed behind her

Joy

The waiter refilled their drinks as
      she laughed and grinned at
      his inappropriate comments
      from across the table
She didn't know it
Or maybe she did
      but
That smile
That giggle
The joy he saw on her face when she
      looked at him
Was going to get her fucked

Collection

To have her open for me
The way she spreads wasps and butterflies
    to pin in her collection

Delicate

My oh so delicate sin
Comprised of heartbeats and skin
        and eyes that stare so deep
Her pale, light complexion
Is porcelain perfection
        in everything I see

Eye Contact

A touch so tender
Lips softer than any she'd ever had placed
      around her nipples
A tongue that seemed to answer her every desire
Fingers that gracefully placed themselves
      everywhere
Giving blissful sensations she
      hadn't ever imagined
Her new lover knew her inside and out
Yet even after the final shudder subsided
      she found it strange to look into her eyes

Work Shirt

Button after button
Adorning her in the blue denim shirt
>   I wear to work
It drapes over her small frame with an
>   unexpected sexiness
Resting on her knees
She reaches and I aid her with the removal
>   of my belt
She devours me with a warmth I have
>   never known
Scraping flints and starting a fire that cannot be
>   calmed with only her mouth
Upon the mattress she is repeatedly
>   tasted
>   enjoyed and
>   filled
After daylight breaks, I drape the denim
>   over my torso
So that throughout my work day
>   I am reminded of her kisses when the
>   collar brushes my neck

And can frequently inhale for the scent
     left by her lust and
     the dreams I may have occupied
     while she slept in my clothing

Before They Started

She swore it was easier to walk
    and that the room was much cooler
    before they had started

Melting

Eyes widened and bright
His hands were a pure delight
Melting from their touch

Sinfully Divine

The flavor she craved was always covering him
    whenever they'd finished
She religiously pushed her lover onto his back
To where she could
    lick him
    suck him
    insert the tip of her tongue into
    the end of him
All while firmly stroking to release his body of
    every single remaining drop
The taste of them was sinfully divine
"This is us"
She thought to herself as she took him fully
    behind her lips
Causing him to helplessly quake
    at her mouths delight

See the Sea

To see the sea with her
Taking her away from the
      toil
      burden and
      heartache she lives every day
To have the waves wash away the pain as they
      lapped at our feet
To watch the sky change and fade into twilight
      around us
Then we might sleep for a single night without
      a care

This Dandelion

So many wishes, dreams
Playful thoughts run through my mind
This dandelion

Summer Storm

She was everything a summer storm could be

As bright upon my eyes as any flash of lightning

Labored breath pushing against my neck like a
    warm, troubled wind

Her cries of saturation were the thunder
    preceding her release

And the rains she brought upon me forced my
    urges to fuck her into bloom

Keys

My hands upon discovered skin were the keys that
      opened her up for me
Intermittent breaths and vocalizations welcomed
      me into her
A place which provided a flavor that still dances
      across my tongue
Now music plays again as I gaze upon
      the empty space in my home
      she occupied the evening before
A desire to once more firmly grip her flesh
      with my hands and
      taste her lust upon my lips
This memory saturating my every thought

Hanging on Me

I smiled before hanging her panties on me
     before we coupled
And to this day
Even though they've been washed
     I grin inside at the thought of how the
     fluids from our
     furious fucking flooded those fibers
     every time I see her wearing them

Hear

When you whisper on
    dark
      silent evenings
I'll still hear you

Winds of March

Winter gives way to spring
The winds of March drag the numbers
    that represent how the air
    feels to us out of its depths
Droplets trickle down you and fall
    towards the ground below
    as you desperately cling
    to what allows you to be
The ground absorbs what it can
The remaining drippings form a puddle
    that you fall into
    before painfully evaporating
While everyone around you celebrates the sunshine
And the fact that you are now only a memory

I Consoled Her

I held her tightly as
     tears soaked my shirt
Heartache at the discovery of
     our son's suicidal thoughts
Moments after, she slept with a married
     high school friend of mine
Crying to me again when he
     committed suicide
     on my birthday

Again, I consoled her

Now I keep my arms around her ex
Waking each day to hopefully
     make it known
That her words aren't as strong as
     he thinks they are
That this world won't be
     better without him

Raindrops

I loved her once
     but never again
A way to cope will find me and
     keep me from her pain
One day her harsh words will be
     carelessly brushed away
     like raindrops hitting my windshield

Facade

Fathomless is the abyss of pain
    that can be hidden
    behind the facade
    of a smile

Cloudy

At the end of the coldest summer I can
      ever remember
Cold in my heart
      not in the air from temperature
Songs heard from birds as flowers and leaves
      decorate each trees
      outstretched fingers
They sing and grow although
I haven't seen the sun in as long as I can remember

On the Windows

Humidity collecting on the windows
    despite the rain being finished for
    quite some time
Similar to the perception of something you love
    after the last tears had fallen
    from your eyes
Never to be seen the same again

Laying a Blanket

Fingers were outstretched towards
    angry
    cloudy and
    ever-lamenting skies
In the hopes that
    the lightning
    would extend toward and
    hold my hand
Laying a blanket of silence over my cries
    with a singular
    reverberating
    thunderous taking of my life

Summer's Door

Steps taken that seemingly led to nowhere
Voices projected conversations about
      years gone by
Metaphoric breezes occasionally whispered into
      each of our ears as the
      first signs of autumn
      boisterously giggled
      beneath the soles
      of our shoes
The air was drier than in days past
The not so distant harvesting of grain added
      a faint scent of the season
      to every breath we inhaled
Crickets chirped in a panic from any dark corners
      they could hide themselves in
Almost as if they were somehow
      instinctively aware
      of the frost that would soon
      settle across the landscape

We kept walking
We kept talking
Completely quiet about the multitudes of
     idiosyncrasies each of us observed
     as we both disliked carrying on
     conversations in parallel
This air
These words
The smiles and heartaches that could only
     be heard
Will surely be remembered each time
     autumn stands outside
     summer's door

Pieces

Golden beauty held by myself as the colors of fall
The once life giving foliage brought to
      rest upon the ground
Just like the leaves torn from their branches
      by the rains of October
I'm still here
Only under your feet
      in pieces

Sympathetic Sky

Rain falls from a sky
     overcast and covered in grey
Thank you for this
I really needed it today

Place in the Line

Cold mornings

Introspection

Reflection

The sky turns blue as I wait until the
      very last minute to exit my vehicle

Another day of trading my time for compensation

Becoming increasingly dissatisfied with my
      place in the line

Bumblebee

Offering her rest from her flight
    I hold out my hand
Warmed by the summer sunshine
    she will hover, lower, and land

Weightless on my palm
    a precious and dangerous thing
I set aside my worry
    knowing that at any moment she could sting

October Pavement

The cool air kisses my face before I fully pull the
    zipper of my jacket above my collarbone

Ears held by the brisk air that surrounds them

Steps taken one by one as the umbrella blooms and
    is held over my head

No music today
Just the constant pattering of raindrops on the
    makeshift roof above me
Accompanied by the splatter of shallow puddles
    and leaves folding underneath the soles
    of my shoes

My mind drifts from daydreams to visions
To hopes and wishes that have been covered by
    dunes of sand that somehow escaped the
    confines of the hourglass that
    once held them

Then my thoughts drift to her

The damp autumn air acts as simply another
        reminder of the gift that she's given me

A sense of accomplishment and purpose

A new perspective on who I am and what I
        am capable of

And I miss her

My heart will always gently cling to the memory
        of her the way fallen pieces of oak, maple
        and sycamore adhere themselves to the
        October pavement

Leaving impressions on the concrete long after the
        season has passed

Morning Moon

I looked at her like a crescent moon suspended
against the sunrise
Trying to observe the darker parts of her that
weren't so easily seen

Fly

Merely a piece of earth
Torn from the soil that held me down for
      uncountable years
Lifted
Touched
Admired for the single smooth side
      that my being contained
The rough of me ignored and unimportant
Cast through the air
      I skipped across her beautiful surface
      with a joy I'd never known

And I drowned in her

Now I lay in the riverbed
Where I can always look up to her and smile
      at the memories of the day that
      I thought I could fly

Bidding Farewell

Few of us took turns shoveling dirt into
    the opening in the ground that
    was now the forever home of
    my mother's mother

As each scoop released its contents
    onto and eventually covering
    the urn below
    we grew more and more silent

We were all saying goodbye to her
    but I also felt as though
    we were bidding farewell to
    the family we once were

The realization manifested that all were being
    kind and respectful to one another
    only to comfort her
    for her last days in our presence

This would soon be ending

I saw the way she faded over those last days
        happen to this group of siblings
        in a matter of minutes as we
        entered our vehicles and drove away

Exiting the gates and entering the roadway
        we drove to the east
        on Highway 2
        making the return trip on winding roads

Vehicles quickly separated as each
        individual family began
        making it back to the places
        they each called home

Streets, cities, and states would soon
        separate all of us while
        some were divided by bridges
        much more difficult to traverse

Another Life

That moment
The one right before dawn when night is
    at its darkest
When the light is low enough to see
    the luminescence of my breaking heart
    crumbling to pieces and falling
    upon the ground
Only to become sands in the hourglass of
    another life

Pillowcases

Watching them walk into where, for years,
    I did reside

Kisses

Smiles

"I love you's" and chipper waving mask the
    heartache that fills me

Driving away to songs I love, but internally
    shuffling my feet as I feel my way along
    the ever darkening path to my home
    away from them

There I lay in the beds I have provided for them
    and cast my tears to their pillowcases

Where the scents of their hair and my emptiness
    collide

Illuminated

A night different than
      so many others
Approaching my home as I could on
      any night
But this evening the windows that so often are
      blank
      dim
      lonely
      desolate
      forlorn
Were illuminated from within
And the thought that my children were
      utilizing that light
Warmed my fucking soul
Because I know that weeks will pass
      before I might see this glow again

Breathing Life

Anger

Frustration

Disappointment in myself for letting
      the thought of wishing my children
      were older carry any merit

I refuse to keep these thoughts alive and

I refuse to forgive her for breathing life into them

Anger

The sun hasn't shined in so many days
How I ache for the warmth
    for the heat
    for the burn
To provide something that my senses can
    focus their anger on

Without

Cold outside, but colder within
Because my children aren't here with me
In my home and in my heart
The first year without a Christmas tree

Skyfall

I awaken to the remnants of rain
Pavement glistening from the overnight skyfall
Mist
Drizzle
Sprinkling enough to still produce the
      pattering
      of water trickling along
      the interior of
      aluminum downspouts
Glossy ground reflecting the gloom of
      a clouded atmosphere
An embrace from the sky
      because she's always known
      my heart

Sparkle

The brighter the light shines
It shortens the life of the filament
      from which it emits
And she has burned so very bright
Illuminating all with such an intensity that
      everyone around her
      has been blinded to the
      irreversible damage
      that has occurred
I'm so afraid that one day I'll witness
      her beautiful sparkle
      become dim

Wings

She was among the most gorgeous of
      butterflies
Before those beauteous wings were taken
      from her
She stayed for so long
Perched on the same stem
      day after day
Feeding from the only flower she had
      ever known
I long for her to crawl upon my finger
So that I might carry her through my garden
      from bloom to bloom
Using a free hand to clear paths through
      the foliage
Allowing her to taste nectar she could never reach
      even with her wings

Deja vu

Her long showers were taken with the
    hope of initiating a rebirth
But when she stepped outside the curtain
    all was deja vu

She

She is tired
She is my lover
She is mine
 and I love her
When my hands touch her face
 and sheets wrap around us
I long for weary eyes to
 close
 relax and
 worry about nothing but
 loving me and letting me
 love her

In These Arms

I'm thankful for the things she's been through
Because I'm seeing her pain for only its charms
Every single person who has ever hurt her
Has led her straight to being
      wrapped in these arms

Anise & Wormwood

Clean and cold
Water trickles over the fruit of the cane
Dragging its grains down from the spoon
      into the glass

The sweetening awakens her loveliness

The green fairy wakes from her slumber to bless
      each sweetened droplet
      as it meets the delightful intoxicant
      that was previously
      kissed
      loved and
      aroused by anise and wormwood

Lay upon me, sweet fairy
Show me all you wish for these eyes to see

Molded

The greatest result of love
    isn't to be changed by someone
But rather
Allowing the beauty of yourself
    to be warmed and
    carefully molded
Perhaps into something that you
    were too afraid
    didn't know you wanted or
    weren't allowed to believe you could
But you found that in their hands
    you could do anything
    enjoy everything and
    be anything you chose

Open Window

Leave your window open at night
        so that my hope for you
        can be carried in on cool, dark breezes
My rustling to drift across dreaming ears
Wifty hands holding sleepy cheeks
        as gentle kisses are
        delicately placed on closed lips and
        a silky forehead
Kisses that bring with them a soothing comfort
        forcing you deeper into
        a blanket wrapped bliss
As an unconscious half smile crawls across
        one of my most favorite of faces
        forcing irises to flutter under
        petal-like eyelids
Eyelids that lift as mornings light fills the room
And your heart swells with the strange feeling
        that you are no longer alone

A Trip Home

We drove for hours
Laughing and making comments about songs that
    we had forgotten even existed
Occasionally kissing the hands we held throughout
    much of our journey
A trip home that neither of us really
    wanted to make
If only we could simply stay away forever
Unfortunately we knew our reappearances were
    necessary
    so we continued on
Finding sympathetic areas of rain and fog that
    seemed to want us to stay on the road
    just a little while longer
The ironic beauty of several bioluminescent deaths
    streaked across the windshield before
    we arrived in the dark hours of morning
That night we slept connected
Each relieved and at the same time disappointed
    that we had to return to the grind of
    our daily lives

Creek

Beside the creek we sit

Feet dangling into warm summer current as
        fingers intertwine and
        conversations flourish

Smiles and laughs

Kisses and playful nibbles are placed on the
        raised knuckles of our interlocked hands

A moment away

Miss You More

When you aren't beside me
I can never decide which miss you more
    my eyes
    my lips or
    my fingertips

Bottle

He wanted to bottle this lover up
     and carry her in his pocket
Making it possible for him to
     kiss
     touch and
     fuck her
     throughout his work day

Art

I painted her skin with palms and fingerprints
Digging in and dragging along her flesh

She had always been art in my eyes
I was just giving her more color

My Flower

It was known between us that she was mine

That the water brought forth from the touch of
my hand and the sunshine emanating from
my gaze would cause her to grow

Blooming with gasps and parted lips whenever she
kissed me

Pretty Little Smile

Sometimes
In the middle of the day
My thoughts become overcome with the desire to
     release myself
      behind that pretty little smile of yours

Until Now

Her eyes shimmered in the photograph
    she sent
A smirk
Flushed cheeks and a brow giving away the fact
    that what she had done to herself
      was a secret
Until now

Obvious

It was obvious that she had missed him
Letting him know with her mouth
    but not being able to speak

Rumbles

She wished me goodnight
    as I did to her
And in our dreams we frolicked under
    warm sunshine and
    cool moonbeams
Making violent love as jealous rumbles of thunder
    begged to be heard just beyond the nearest
    window pane

Sleepless, Restless

She would lay there awake at night
Wandering hands welcomed warmly between
     widely open legs
A slick finger on each side of her epicenter
     sliding from fingertips to palm
     before diving into herself
An arched back forces a turned cheek deep
     into the pillow
As delightful gasps dance across her tongue and
     past her lips
A free hand
     grips
     grasps and
     squeezes a breast
Pulling the nipple with the
     simulated amount of force
     he applied with his teeth before
     using the same hand to
     slap her moaning mouth
The way she wished he would
     when he fucked her there

Whispers

Laying her back onto the softest of bedsheets
    I request that her eyes remain closed
Kissing from the tip of her nose across the most
    adorable of cheeks
Watching to ensure closed eyelids
    my lips apply the softest of affections
    to her ears
    before whispering
    the filthiest of fantasies into them
Soft hands attempt to slide under cotton panties
    to push against
    the ache growing inside of her
I take those tender wrists and
    restrain them at her sides
    as the lightly spoken sins
    fall from my tongue
    into an ear that has never wanted to
    hear so much
Cheeks flush
Eyelids flutter and struggle to keep the darkness
    over her retinas

Legs close tightly as she rocks herself
    softly and deeply
Writhing in the wish that
    someone
    something
    anything
    touch her there as a tear rolls down
    the side of her
    ever reddening complexion
A token of lust from the pain of desire
    piercing her being

Bookmark

I placed myself across her tongue
    as a bookmark
So that I could always start on my favorite page

Greetings

The best greetings end in
     the impatient removal of clothing
Followed by her eyes looking up at me
While the amount of "Hello"
     I give that isn't swallowed
     rolls down her chest

Dousing

The first signs of the impending day approach
Nautical twilight
The gradual fading of the stars
    announces her arrival
She glows and swaddles me in her warmth
Shining so brightly that I can never truly gaze
    upon her beauty
So I close my eyes
I slowly exhale and let her heat permeate the
    skin of my face
Eyelids remain tight as I invite the
    dousing of my body
      with her fire

She Would Have

Her lips parted
Ever so slowly did he slide across her
    tongue as they closed around him
    before descending to where hair
    gently greeted her face
She took a long breath
Taking in the scent of what makes him a man
    before pushing him against the back
    of her throat
A vigorous shudder was
    involuntarily extracted from him
    as her voice
    deeply and
    lustfully
    penetrated the senses of the
    skin held against her tongue
Hands desperately pushed through her hair
    in an attempt to slow what was
    happening to him
A near scream leapt from his mouth
    as he filled hers
And if it were possible for her to smile
    she would have

Devotions

With my hand in hers
      she led me into her sanctuary
There she disrobed
Slowly leaning forward
      facing away from me
Her arms rested on the mattress when she
      asked to hear my devotions
Her words spoken in a voice that gently
      drifted away from us
Being most devout
      I fell to my knees behind her
      used careful hands to open the delicate
      holy texts
      placed my lips against her
      and I prayed

Breath Away

The way he moved
The way he exhaled nervously
She used her mouth on his
      as her friend used hers elsewhere
She knew what he was feeling
Her sensitive lips read his sensations as their
      tongues danced together
Keeping her mouth to his
Her friend emptied him of his lust
      while she took his breath away

Just Me

Burying my nose in the empty pillowcase
    next to mine
All in the hope that I could somehow
    inhale the comfort that settles here
    on the nights she spends in my bed

But it's just me

And I lay awake with my thoughts
Thoughts of how warm her skin becomes
    while she sleeps
The sound of her breathing as an
    unconscious mind displays a scene for her
    that only she can see
Perhaps my hands would wander and rouse her
Perhaps the sliding of my palms along
    the skin of her leg would transition to
    fingers finding themselves held to her
    under the elastic owned by adorable panties

Maybe she would awaken and turn to me
        wrists connecting behind my neck
Our lips would meet and eventually part
        allowing our
        tacky
        tired mouths
        to taste how sleepy we really were
I would find myself settling between her legs
        blood engorging me
        my body begging for hers
She would pull her panties aside as I found my way
        through the opening of my boxer briefs
Upon our coupling I would find her
Warm
Smooth
Slightly more viscous than usual
        as I nearly withdrew before slowly
        bringing our bodies together
        over and over
Our undergarments happily embracing
        one another
So much more silence than in times past
No sounds but our breathing and
        the occasional vehicle driving by
        on the street outside

She noticed the familiar stuttering
    of my movements before
    breaking the silence

"Yes...yes...please cum inside me."

There would be no way to stop from
    emptying myself at the sound of her
    invitation
We'd kiss as her body coaxed mine into giving
    all I possibly could before I released myself
    from her embrace
The elastic of her soaked panties
    making an effort to
    keep me from leaving by gripping
    the left side of my cock
She would turn to lay on her right side as I settled
    in behind her
An arm reaching around that she held
    against a breast
I would kiss the hair separating her neck
    from my lips before we slipped into
    unconsciousness
Somehow both dreaming the same dream

Unknowingly smiling in our sleep

But it's just me

Next Best Thing

What time is it?
　　I ask myself
The quiet coolness of what must be
　　the early hours of a new day
　　envelopes everything with
　　its darkness
Another night I lay wide awake
Sleep and rest becoming a mere
　　plaything of hope
I turn to her
　　silently sleeping under
　　sheets and blankets
Underneath which I softly run my hand
　　over a delightfully naked ass
　　and pepper her bare shoulders with
　　the most tender of kisses
Because if I am not to dream
　　I'll treat my lips and fingertips to
　　the next best thing

Intensity

She was dying for her skin to
Sting
Burn
Break and
Bleed for him
Dying for intensity that would follow her
throughout the coming days
So that she could feel as though his
grip was on her still pink ass
even when they were miles away
from one another
Her skin begged to be loved in a way
that would take longer to heal
than the time they would be apart

Sunrise

Arms raised as my fingers pulled the cotton
    garment that kept her covered higher

Over her head and onto the floor

Eyes met
Only for mine to drift and feed eager retinas
    with the sight of the
    beautiful nakedness before them

Like they were seeing a sunrise for the
    very first time

Polaris

Wrapping fingers around her Achilles
Thumbs push and swirl under the arch of her foot
The sensation of his skillful grip leads to pleasure
    as the pressure is released
Presenting himself as an artisan
    delving into the joy of his craft
    as he worked diligently at her feet
Hands meander toward higher muscles as these are
    kneaded and shaped into bliss
    behind her mind's eye
Palms cast their light upon rounded knees
    as she breathes
And with a locked gaze legs part and
    the guiding shine of Polaris
    leads welcomed touches even further north

In Return

Her back beautifully adorned by the pink
    my desire decorated such pale skin with
Nearly pure recreations of my hands on each side
    of the ass I love to
    squeeze
    spank and
    grab while I work
She turns and as she lays I gaze into those eyes
I lay a hand upon her deeply breathing chest and
    explore her skin
Finding nipples that all but leap between my
    fingertips before I
    clutch
    pull and
    twist them
She gasps
An adorable, rosy-cheeked, freshly fucked smile
    frolics across her face
    warming me
And I smile in return

Silhouette

We lay together naked
    uncovered and
    physically exposed to one another after
    falling to the sheets

Sweat lingers

Breathing slows

My fingers gliding along the silhouette laid before
    my eyes as we speak

Open

Honest

Lips and tongues meet more times than could
    be counted

She runs her hands through my hair and
    I close my eyes
    smile and
    drown in the joy of the moment

My Princess

Shimmering

The light refracting and reflecting countless lights
as my position to her changes

Glimmering azure flickered as she donned an
entirely new style of ornament

Worn in a place no man had decorated her before

I pushed into her slowly, greeted with an exotic
pressure

A new embrace

Given to me from her after crowning this beauty
as my princess

New Jerusalem

There is a heaven that's not to be found
    above our heads or
    in the skies
New Jerusalem appears when you explore
    her heart and mind
Before tasting and penetrating the gates
    between her thighs

Envelope

Enclosing checks

Affixing postage

My thoughts drift to her each time my wet tongue
touches an envelope

Sweetness

She blessed my hands with the sweetness
of her wettest kisses
Despite our tongues never parting

The Warmth

Reluctantly her eyes did close
She wanted them to see, but he firmly requested
    that her lashes rest on her cheeks
She waited
Kneeling
Listening
The sounds of a quiet shuffling and his
    increasingly labored breathing
    filled her ears
Almost instinctively, her jaw dropped slightly
Seconds before she felt the warmth land on her lips
Her heart pounded at the thought of the bliss she
    hoped he was feeling
She opened her eyes for the shortest of moments
    to catch a glimpse of his hand
    slowly approaching
Her eyes closed again and she tried
    to keep from smiling
    as his fingers met her face
Fingers that moved with the same determined
    fluidity contained in the liquid he pushed
    towards her mouth

Over her lips and past her teeth
Onto a tongue that was dying for the flavor she
associated
with his adoration for her
Her mouth closed around his fingers
Firmly drawing the taste of his raw desire to
the back of her throat
Repeatedly did she partake as his hands delivered
the release that her skin had collected
Against his wishes her eyes fully opened
Looking up
Admiring him
Taking in the tender gaze of his face as she
greedily sucked from his fingers
His eyes were filled with satisfaction
Content he had provided her with something
only she was allowed to taste
Fulfilled by the thought that she was nourished
with what he was dying to feed her

Sunflowers

The sunflowers turned so that they could
      stay in her light
I often found myself doing the same
Who could resist such
      brilliance and warmth?
And oh, how she could make me grow

Milk

Kitten loved to be held in his grip

To be brought to purr repeatedly by the
    touch of his hands

To feel the heat of his lust roll from her
    collarbone down over
    her breasts

But most of all

She craved her master's hand
    sliding along where his fluid
    would flow
    before placing his filled palm
    up to open lips
So kitten's tongue could embrace the flavor
    of her favorite milk

Blustered

There were times when the wind would blow
and the air blustered around
the skin of her neck
Forcing memories of the kisses and love bites
he once placed there
to be rustled like piles of autumn leaves

Around Us

The pinpoints of light that hung in the sky
    kissed her skin with visibility
A graceful silhouette provided by the glorious
    luminescence of the newly
    waning moon
She leans forward
Granting me a taste of the stars
    in the form of a breast
    pushing past my lips
Her hand is felt on the inside of my knee
She moves her fingers ever forward
And with a deliberate grip
    the myriad of universes that
    allowed me to see her
    seemed to helplessly fall around us

Entranced

I sit and sip

Absinthe crosses my lips as she sleeps

Sheets and blankets cover the bruised and
      pinkened skin I left her with

"Please"

"Yes"

"Thank you"

Statements that echo in my memory as images
     of the flogger falls landing upon her delicate
     skin replay again and again in my mind

I watch the linens rise and fall with every breath
     she breathes and become entranced

Holding my respirations between each of hers

Elixir

She knelt between his spread legs
     asking him to lay back and
     to remain motionless
While he did she sucked upon him greedily
     as if she needed relief from some
     unknown affliction
And what she could drink of him
     was the elixir that would
     bring her soul some comfort
Unknowingly curing them both

Zipper

Each click brought from separated zipper teeth
    gave me life
More of her back showing with each
    passing moment
    as I freed her body from the
    form fitting dress
    that covered her
I drowned my eyes with the sight of her now
    uncovered spine
    before releasing its tether
Hanging on her shoulders
What was once so incredibly sexy
    became benign and lifeless against the
    treasure of her fair skin
Without clinging to her
    it was nothing but cloth
The iconic sound of a gown dropping to the floor
    reverberated through my being
Without a spoken syllable from either of us
    she placed knees and then elbows
    on the floor

Resting her adorable head on her
      crossed forearms
Now on display in front of me
      bare ankles and
      shoeless feet began to slowly separate
      from one another
      beautifully presenting her upturned vagina
Clearly an invitation that would not be denied
Just the sight of her thickened the air
      that seemed to be harder and harder
      to breathe
There she was
Exposed and ready for the taking

Giggles

Floating above her on the
   sound of her laughter
   as she giggles at an oddly timed
   thought
My lips curve and open as
   the smile on my face meets hers
The pressure of her body
   tensing and releasing
   around me as I soften inside of her
I hope with all of the heart in my chest
   that the memory of
   her smiling face
   her voice and
   her body laughing against mine
Never leaves my mind

Divinity

Stars sparkled behind her eyelids as
    he took her there
    over and over again
A jealous god watched from afar
    as a human with an awareness of sin
    that couldn't possibly be known
Provided her with a heaven
    his divinity would never allow

End of the Sky

Meet me at the end of the sky
Where the
    land
    sea and
    air become one and we'll do the same
The horizon will be ours while a
    new earth is formed
Where the
    light
    dark and
    in between can be used for us without shame

Leaves

Her cheek nestled into the warmth
        of his blanket while she
        lifted an eager backside
His hands found their way from the
        backs of bent knees
        moving higher and higher
Fingers pushed into the flesh covering
        her beautiful behind
        before spreading and
        placing his lips within the
        division he had created
Kisses landed upon her hidden places
        the same way
        autumn's colored leaves
        devote themselves to the ground

Intermittent

Hearts resting after the fluids had flown
Whispers and kisses felt by tired skin
Eyes that left each other's gaze only to
      blink or capture one another's nakedness
Fingers trace her form
Gently weaving from exposed skin to where we had
      just released ourselves
Hot and damp as I had left her
Smiles and softly expressed affections lead to desire
      and a question
"I wish you could stay."
"Would you?"
The light did cease but sleep took time and was
      intermittent
As each time I woke I
      affixed a kiss
      caressed a breast and
      brought an arm around to hold her close
Because on their own
      the dreams behind my eyelids
      weren't enough to grant me rest

Belt

Through multiple loops
Buckled
Benign

When removed from his pants
That same belt knew her most secret desires
More than her closest friends

Off Guard

She was caught off guard
As the memory of the stings suddenly made her
    as wet as the moment they were delivered

With Open Eyes

She watched his eyes close as he
     emptied himself
His expression
     hearing him breathe
     feeling him throb as he filled her
Sweetly smiling
     she truly believed that she was
     dreaming with open eyes

Thankful

Sitting next to him on the sofa
      as the aroma of the impending holiday meal
      filled her senses
Slowly she stroked the inside of his pant leg
      from the knee to where
      what was underneath his jeans
      provided an increasingly firm place for
      her fingers to explore
All she could think of was how she longed
      for him to drop her pants
      in the next room
      give her the stuffing she craved and
      something to truly be thankful for

Pain

She begged me to hurt her
Proclaiming that when I did
    it wasn't pain that she felt

The Time He Took

The time he took was torture
Holding himself over her body
Softly stroking her with the end of his
    clock's minute hand
Tapping on the center of her open legs
The ticking of the seconds felt like hours
    as she watched his eyes for the
    days to pass
He but dipped into her sea of eternity
Gently moving around her inner workings
    with only the tip disappearing before
Laying into her and fully
    experiencing her years
Holding still as forever seemed to pass
Soaking him, her time had finally come
And how beautifully did she seem
    to age before his eyes

As I Drive

Her sexy giggles
    make me feel so alive
One hand on the wheel
    while she moans and sucks my fingers
    as I drive

And We Dance

Music plays around us as I
    slowly undress her
Kisses land upon a soft neck as my fingers
    easily undo the clasps that rest over her spine
Hands joyously explore her now braless back
    before the garment is
    tossed to the floor and I pull her to me
Nipples stiffen against my shirt as
    arms intertwine
    lips meet
    and we dance

Calligraphy

Days pass and the marks fade
Skin that was once under my hand
      and between my teeth
      regains its fair complexion
Your flesh cleans its slate
      secretly longing for me to
      once again adorn your body
      with purple and pink
      calligraphy

Bookshelf

The memories of her lovers were
     stacked on shelves like
     cherished novels
There they would stay until the moment
     she needed them
Perhaps a blanket covered afternoon
     on a cold winter's day
     would be the perfect time to
     wipe the dust from their covers

Oasis

Pinned to the mattress
     with my hands around her throat
Using the structure that brings air
     from her kissable lips
     to the lungs that gasp for me
     as my support
I repeatedly push into her open legs
     with all the weight of my being
When finished I stand
Looking down
Admiring the puddle that reaches from
     underneath her
An oasis of fuck in the desert of her duvet

Someone Unknown

All was black to her after the scarf had been tied
    around her eyes
She loved that this forced her to
    feel

    taste

    smell and

    hear

    more than she ever could while using sight
With hands interlocked she followed and was
    led to kneel
Closing her mouth around what touched her lips
    she noticed that his ridges had
    a different feel and
    taste on her tongue
A confused whimper radiated from her before she
    felt the breath and
    heard the voice
    of her lover whispering into her ear

"Shhh. Keep going, my dear"

Her nerves only calmed when the familiar scent
      of her man's hand embraced her nose
She nearly flooded herself at the thought of
      him using his grip to aid her lips
All while someone unknown provided her
      with something to swallow

Teaspoon

Strange winter lightning illuminated the sky
Trying in vain to match the ferocity of the thunder
    that escaped her lips as her face was buried
    into my shoulder
Flooded streets were a teaspoon to the ocean
    brought forth as my hands demanded the
    attention of her body through her clothing

The Falls

With each landing of the falls her body would
      grip tighter and tighter to the false phalluses
      he had slid into her
She fought harder than ever against her instincts
      to proclaim her love for him
As the waves of stings raised pink slivers
      from her skin
      coloring her beautifully lifted backside

Holy Water

Fingers dipped into her baptistery before I was
    blessed by her gasp-laden prayers
A flowing that contained
    so much more redemption
    than the river Jordan rippled with
Before John devoutly baptized his savior there

Drives Home

Lips curve into a smile as
      she turns the car through a bend
      in the road
His scent still filling her nose
His flavor still on her tongue
She drives with her left hand on the
      steering wheel
      elbow at the window while
      a song she loves plays
Her right hand gropes at jeans
      as what he left inside of her
      gently finds its way to where
      fingers can't quite reach
The drives home were one of her favorite things

Crimson

It was barely there
  but she noticed
The discovery of crimson memories
  that remained on the glass
  she was drinking from
  brought a devilish smile
  to her red lips
She looked at him
And when she did her mind began to
  calculate
How much it hurt that she needed
  to wait until after dinner
  to leave lipstick stains around him
  while enjoying the dessert
  he would surely fill her mouth with

Braille

I treated her body as if I were blind
Reading the love notes her flesh wrote for me
    using only my hands

Spin

His eyes meeting hers
    took the world away
His lips on her skin
    made her see stars while
His hand in her panties
    forced them to spin

Under the Blindfold

The darkness brought her salvation
    freedom to release
    to be who she wished she was
The delicious whore for her lover to
    use and devour
To suck and fuck with an absolute lack of
    boundaries and inhibitions
Under the blindfold she was in love with
    the deity she became
Under the blindfold she was free

Snow Angel

On her back

Arms waving, legs extended

Each moving as far as her body would allow

"Do you like my angel?" She giggled while asking

"Yes, but I love your devil." Was my reply

New & Clean

She wrapped her arms around his waist and
    buried her nose into his shoulder
The smell of his freshly washed body
The slight stickiness of his still damp skin
His hair remaining unkempt and
    slightly spiky
The man in her arms was so new and clean
    but all she could think about
    was how dirty her body was
    begging to make him

Sanctuary

Sunlight shone through the stained glass windows
Colors the naked eye couldn't see
    without her naked presence
    before them
The stiffening adornments of these
    cathedral walls
    presented themselves to
    my sight and examination
I came to reflect
I came to pray
I came to worship her
To accept her salvation and
    to be saved
The reverberations of her voice echoing through
    this darkened sanctuary
    allowed for my passage into the light

Pout

My fingers slowly glided along her jawline
   gathering any stray droplets of my lust
   that may have missed her hungry mouth
Lips parted almost involuntarily as
   I drew nearer to them
Her tongue extended slightly
   expecting to free my fingerprints
   of their collection
But just before her sweet tongue could taste
   I used my own to clean them
How absolutely adorable it is to see
   a grown woman pouting
Regardless of her claims to the contrary

Kitten

She approached him on all fours
Reserved
Observant
A stray who desperately needed food
He filled her mouth with flavors
      that had only resided in the
      darkest corners
      of her imagination
His touch
Hands leading to places she was at one time
      hesitant of intrusion

But now as his kitten she welcomed him

Sensations forced her backside
      high into the air
As she stroked his pant leg with her cheek
And uncontrollably purred
      at his feet

Powerful and Weak

But she loved the way sucking him
  made her tingle
  made her ache
  made her wet
She persuaded him to cum into her loving mouth
  with the motion of her hand
While the guttural groans she extracted from
  his throat
  somehow made her feel powerful
And yet
  in the same moment
  it made her weak

Taste of Hell

Addicted to the way you kiss me
To the divinity of your soft lips meeting mine
    and to the taste of Hell on your tongue

Share a Snowflake

The street was busier than would have
     been expected
Our soles land upon a sidewalk that was
     no longer visible
     as boot covered feet make
     footprint after footprint
An ever growing trail built upon the memories
     of countless footsteps
Eventually blanketed with invisibility by the
     rapidly falling snow
My gloved hand gently squeezes the
     mitten in its grasp
     before I turn
     look into your eyes and
     ask if you'd like to share a snowflake
     before smiling and
     holding out my tongue

To My Throat

Not a word was spoken
Still her wanton vocalizations landed upon
    my ears
Almost as if they were a knife held
    to my throat
Letting me know that the touch of my hands
    wouldn't be enough to satisfy
    her desires

Prism

She swore he was a prism of a man
He caused color after color to
    run through her mind
Thoughts and desires of things she had never
    wanted to experience
Because all the light that came before him
    was cold and white

Assembled

The angel she was had fallen
    into the arms of the
    devil he is
The lust she had swallowed
The spaces in her angelic form she
    allowed
    desired
    begged him to occupy
    damned her
The sins they committed were the foundation
    of the heaven
    they had assembled for themselves

Blur & Twinkle

Eyes fixed on the way his fingernails
    expertly disassembled the
    tape
    ribbons and
    wrapping paper
    she had used to disguise
    her present for him
How she would have loved to
    lay her head on the skirt
    underneath the tree and
    stare through the artificial branches
While a much more impatient version
    of his fingers
    tore away the covering of her gift box
Forcing the festive lights in her eyes to
    blur and twinkle

Everywhere

One door
One window
One armless wooden chair
One humble bookshelf with few more than
     a dozen entries
And yet this place still roused memories of
     an old library
This was her first time here in what
     seemed to be ages
But her mind wandered through the thought
     of this place daily

She took the top rail of the chair in her hands and
     slowly began positioning its feet
     over distorted circles worn into the
     weathered hardwood
The back turned towards the window
The seat facing the door
She began to undress
     laying her clothes haphazardly
     in the corner

She stood naked in front of the window
     allowing the warmth from the sunshine
     to cascade over all of the skin within
     its reach
She happily sighed and stepped away
     bare feet taking her towards the chair
Standing in front of it
     she closed her eyes while an exhale
     that lasted slightly longer than usual
     exited a pair of lungs that were dying
     to become intoxicated with a much more
     intense intake of oxygen
Hands held onto the chair while
     one at a time
     her knees were brought to rest at the
     back of the padded seat frame
     while her arms crossed along the
     top slat that brought the sides together
Laying her face onto her arms
She sighed
She smiled and
She waited

Who knows how long she knelt in that seat
Her skin exposed
Her bare ass thoroughly enjoying its freedom
The shadow of a cloud darkened the window
     once
     twice
     or was that a third...
     she hadn't kept count
The heart inside of her skipped a beat when
     the ears that held back
     her shoulder length
     blonde hair
     told her that the creaking
     from the doorknob was him

At first
     the footsteps reverberating from each
     step on the
     hardwood floor were the only indication
     he had entered the room
Air brushed the soles of her bare feet
     before wafting along her timid labia
     and pushing the scent of old books
     into her nose
     as he closed the door

The click and snap of the latch
     made her smile

It was all she could do to restrain herself from
     giggling when she felt a hand on the
     left side of her ass
     then another on the right
She stared straight ahead at the window
     as he held her open
     and his breath
     slowly began to make its way
     closer and closer
The ache contained in the desire for his
     mouth to make contact was mutual
But he just stared
Breathing close enough to persuade her skin
     to become riddled with thousands of
     standing hairs
She did her best to keep the initial shiver contained
     as his lips finally touched her
Small pecks of kisses were preceded by
     the welcomed
     brushing of his beard against her
     newly shaved skin
Starting low

His kisses so gently ascending from where a
    clitoris remained covered
    to where he could have easily slid
    a wet tongue into her
Higher yet to where his slightly puckered lips
    rested against her ass
There they stayed in contact while he quietly
    hummed a single drawn out note
A pang grew inside of her at a depth she
    didn't know existed
A growl she didn't intend to be audible nearly
    shook her with the accidental volume
    it was presented with

He giggled semi-maliciously before separating his
    body from hers

The absence of his lips against her skin, and the
    few footsteps she heard soon after
    nearly saddened her
    as she watched him walk to the
    side of the room

He returned and stood between her and
    the window

The shadow he cast robbed her skin of the
        ultraviolet warmth the afternoon sun
        had been giving her

It took a few seconds for her eyes to adjust and
        when they did she saw him standing
        with a neatly folded sheet in his hands
He began to turn it over and over
        and as he did the linen made its way
        to the floor before he spread his arms
        as far as he could
A corner between each thumb and forefinger
With a fluid motion he raised his arms
        and for a second she could see that
        he was pants-less
The bottom button of his shirt and the tip
        of his neck tie almost completely obscured
        him
But for a moment after the cloth lifted she saw him
        and was instantly starving
As the sheet landed it covered everything he could
        see of her

All her eyes could see were the shades of beige
       that seemed to lighten and darken
       as he proceeded to walk around her
       in circles
He felt for her chin and pulled her jaw open
It was then he tucked a handful of the cotton
       into her mouth to keep it over her eyes

She was now an apparition to him and the world
       she once knew was a ghost
His hands were instantly everywhere
At the times her mind let her think during the lull
       of her body's excitement she wondered
       how the hell one man's touch could
       cover so much of her at once
The masked cupping of her breasts led a
       more and more deliberate grabbing
       and an assertive grip on her nipples
       that she swore she could somehow
       feel between her legs
During several quasi-painful moments she thought
       he wanted to take handfuls of her with him
The grip
The pressure
The spankings

The masked sensation of his fingernails dragging
    down her back and over her ass to descend
    her legs were littered with tiny moments of
    nothing
The immeasurable split seconds
    he wasn't touching her flickered like a strobe

Resting on his knees behind covered legs
Fingers wrapped around her right ankle
Ascending her bare leg
All with a grip that left her with no doubt
    as to where his hand was at any point
    along its journey
A thumb wandered between folds of the
    softest flesh
Simultaneously a finger from his left hand
    gathered and easily inserted a
    small amount
    of cloth into her vagina
His thumb pushed in along with the sheet
    collecting a covering indicative of the
    flooding that must also be breaching
    the weakening levee of her self control
This thumb turned and circled while intermittently
    sliding up and down along the skin
    that guided him

Slowly she began to rock her body up and down
     against the stride of his touch
A low groan developed into a near howl as she
     erratically bucked against him
His eyes gazed in awe as the sheet that was
     tucked into her began to darken
Wicking her lust outward
     beyond the epicenter of her arousal
The moisture moving along the folds of fabric
Her cum crawling through the threads presented
     a visual similar to a morning glory
     opening for
     rain
     sunlight and
     visits from dedicated pollinators

Hands moved and released her from the
     confinement of his touch
He stood
He took steps that led to where he could relieve
     her mouth from the improvised gag
Lifting the sheet over her head revealed a face
     overloaded with exhaustion and desire
But the eyes were still hungry

Filled with a beauty he had never seen amidst the
        emotional emaciation they burned with
How could he deny her?
Running the length of his forefinger along the tip
        of his throbbing erection he gathered the
        liquid that was collecting and practically
        begging to drop towards the floor
Eye contact was made and she sucked the
        urge to fuck that his body couldn't contain
        from the topography of his fingerprints
Waiting a moment longer had been removed
        from any unspoken list of options
Taking a stance behind her
He began to pull on the sheet to reveal the
        beautiful
        sight of the abstract yet somehow
        impressionistic art
        that had been made by the determination
        of his touch
She seductively rotated her once again naked ass
        as much as she could while keeping her
        knees firmly planted toward the
        back of the seat
Almost as if she was taunting him

He looked down at the
       aching
       pulsing
       engorged piece of him sticking through the
       flaps that were lower than any standard
       button pattern could ever keep closed
After dragging his fingers across a tongue that
       was an acting reservoir
He polished his
       stiff
       eager prick to a gleaming shimmer
       before speaking
"My dear, I'm going to fuck you everywhere."
After hearing his statement she defiantly giggled
       before responding
"Yes, please. Everywhere."

Adoration

The shuddering of her body
    under mine
Brought from me an adoration only comparable
    to the way butterflies look at flowers

Thank you.

As always, I would like to thank all of the wonderful friends and family who support me. There are too many to name and my gratitude can never be fully conveyed.

I would like to send a very special thanks to Brooke for editing and checking my grammar, and to Alex at ABC Design for the outstanding cover art. It is absolutely beautiful.

And last, but certainly not least, I would like to thank Sara for brightening my days and blessing me with the comfort of her embrace.

Also available through
Amazon Kindle Direct Publishing

Printed in Great Britain
by Amazon

37991811R00118